SCARY PLACES

Haunted Hotels

by Sarah Parvis

Consultant: Troy Taylor
President of the American Ghost Society

BEARPORT
PUBLISHING

New York, New York

Credits

Cover and Title Page, © Slim Plantagenate/Alamy, © James Steidl/istockphoto.com, and © Lou Oates/istockphoto.com; 4, © Harris Schiffman/Shutterstock; 5, © mediacolor's/Alamy; 6, © Amy Lambert; 7L, © Steven Langerman/Alamy; 7R, © Underwood Photo Archives/SuperStock; 8, © Lake County Museum/CORBIS; 9, Taken circa 1892-in the public domain; 10, © Ron Avery/SuperStock; 11, © Picture Post/Hulton Archive/Getty Images; 12, © Catherine Karnow/CORBIS; 13, © Corbis/SuperStock; 14, Courtesy of Library of Congress Prints and Photographs Division; 15, © Greg Ward/Rough Guides/Alamy; 16, © Michael Tobin; 17, © Michael Tobin; 18, © David Noble Photography/Alamy; 19, © Les Gibbon/Alamy; 20, © Walter Bibikow/Jon Arnold Images/Photolibrary; 21, © Corbis/SuperStock; 22L, Courtesy of The Olde Angel Inn/Lynne Gill; 22R, © North Wind Picture Archives/Alamy; 23T, © Shvaygert Ekaterina/Shutterstock; 23B, © Michael Jenner/Alamy; 24, © Ian Leonard/Alamy; 25L, The Granger Collection, New York; 25R, © Erik Lam/Shutterstock; 26, © Springfield Underground Inc., Courtesy Springfield Greene County Public Library; 27, © Hugh Threlfall/Alamy.

Publisher: Kenn Goin
Editorial Director: Adam Siegel
Creative Director: Spencer Brinker
Design: Dawn Beard Creative
Photo Researcher: Beaura Kathy Ringrose

Library of Congress Cataloging-in-Publication Data

Parvis, Sarah E.
 Haunted hotels / by Sarah Parvis ; consultant, Troy Taylor.
     p. cm. — (Scary places)
 Includes bibliographical references and index.
 ISBN-13: 978-1-59716-574-7 (library bdg.)
 ISBN-10: 1-59716-574-3 (library bdg.)
 1. Haunted hotels—Juvenile literature. I. Title.

 BF1474.5.P37 2008
 133.1'22—dc22
                                    2007043833

For more information, write to Bearport Publishing Company; Inc., 101 Fifth Avenue, Suite 6R, New York, New York, 10003. Printed in the United States of America.

10 9 8 7 6 5 4

Contents

For most people, a hotel room is a place to stay during a vacation. After a few days, guests usually check out and return home. Some people, however, check into a hotel and never check out! Their ghosts stay on, sharing their rooms with the living.

In the 11 haunted hotels in this book, you'll discover the ghost of a bride who never saw her wedding day, a mysterious **spirit** who enjoys pulling the hair of female guests, and a room so haunted that no one is allowed to stay there anymore. So the next time you stay in a hotel, beware! You may not be the only guest in the room.

A Gambler with a Grudge

St. James Hotel, Cimarron, New Mexico

From the 1860s to the 1890s, New Mexico was part of America's Wild West. With few sheriffs, and even fewer laws, it is no surprise that **outlaws** liked to live there. Many who were handy with a **pistol** stayed at the St. James Hotel, including Jesse James and Billy the Kid. While these dangerous **gunslingers** are now long dead, the ghost of one angry customer still makes trouble at the St. James Hotel.

St. James Hotel

In 1901, the owners of the St. James Hotel decided to replace its roof. Imagine their surprise when they found more than 400 bullet holes in the ceiling. This historic hotel had certainly had more than its share of gunfights—and murders.

One unlucky victim was the gambler Thomas James Wright. He was shot in the back after winning the hotel in a poker game. He dragged himself into room 18 and slowly bled to death.

Since then, Wright's angry spirit is said to shove anyone who sets foot in "his" room. So the hotel owners now keep the haunted room locked. No guests are allowed to sleep there anymore.

Every Halloween the owners of the St. James Hotel pour a glass of whiskey for Wright's ghost and leave it in his room. The next morning it is always gone.

Who Was Kate Morgan?

Hotel Del Coronado, Coronado, California

Kate Morgan checked into the Hotel Del Coronado in November 1892. She was supposed to meet her husband there. Five days later, she was found dead on the stairs behind the hotel. Who killed her? Unless Kate's ghost starts talking, no one will ever know.

Hotel Del Coronado

Kate Morgan and her husband, Tom, were gamblers. In the late 1880s they traveled around the country by train winning money in card games. By 1892, however, Kate had had enough. She told her husband that she wanted to stop their life of gambling. So she left Tom and checked into the Hotel Del Coronado.

Tom had agreed to meet Kate at the hotel for Thanksgiving. Yet he never arrived. Kate was found shot in the head five days later. The police were sure she had killed herself. Others believe that her husband sneaked into town and murdered her.

Since Kate's death, strange things have happened in the room where she stayed. Guests have heard voices when no one else is around. Some have seen curtains move when there is no breeze. Others have even spotted the ghost of a woman staring out the window, as if waiting for someone. Perhaps Kate is still hoping Tom will arrive.

Kate Morgan

The light over the steps where Kate's body was found will not stay lit. When the bulb is replaced, it quickly burns out again.

9

The Gray Ghost

Queen Mary Floating Hotel, Port of Long Beach, California

The *Queen Mary* first set sail in 1936. This fancy **ocean liner** was bigger, faster, and more powerful than the *Titanic*. It crossed the Atlantic Ocean more than 1,000 times. During World War II (1939–1945), the ship was painted gray and used by the **military**. "The Gray Ghost" carried more than 800,000 soldiers, including 16,683 in one trip. Her speed and size helped save thousands of soldiers. Unfortunately, they killed some, too.

The *Queen Mary*

In October 1942, the *Queen Mary* and the H.M.S. *Curacao* were traveling together during World War II for protection. To avoid enemy torpedoes, the two ships zigzagged in the ocean at set times. When the *Curacao* mistakenly turned at the wrong time, the *Queen Mary* sliced the smaller ship in half. The *Curacao* sank quickly. About 330 men died before help arrived.

In 1967, the *Queen Mary* stopped making trips. She was permanently **docked** at Long Beach, California, and was turned into a hotel. The ghosts of the *Curacao*'s doomed sailors, however, still haunt the ship. Members of the hotel staff have heard the sound of rushing water and banging noises near the part of the *Queen Mary* that hit the *Curacao*. Some even claim to hear the screams of the *Curacao*'s dying crew echoing throughout the hotel.

The sinking of the *Curacao* was not the only deadly accident caused by the *Queen Mary*. On July 10, 1966, John Pedder, an 18-year-old crew member, was crushed to death by one of the ship's heavy doors. His ghost has since been seen near the engine room wearing dirty blue overalls.

Party on the 13th Floor

Biltmore Hotel, Coral Gables, Florida

The Biltmore Hotel was built for $10 million in 1926. At the time, it was **illegal** to make or sell alcohol in the United States. Yet that didn't stop the Biltmore. The 13th floor of the hotel was home to a **speakeasy**. It also had a **casino**. As a result, a number of **gangsters** went to the 13th floor to drink and gamble. One of them is still having a good time there.

Biltmore Hotel

Thomas "Fatty" Walsh was a Florida gangster. He worked with many criminals. He also made a lot of enemies. In 1929, he was shot and killed on the 13th floor of the Biltmore Hotel.

Even in death, however, Fatty seems to want to keep the party going at the Biltmore. According to some guests, the lights in the hotel's elevator suddenly turn on and off. The elevator passes the guests' floor and goes straight to the 13th floor.

One woman who was taken to the empty floor said she smelled cigars burning. She called out, but no one answered. She heard the sound of laughter, even though no one was there. Somehow, the party never ends for Thomas "Fatty" Walsh—the ghostly gangster.

One guest riding in the Biltmore's elevator made the mistake of saying that Fatty got what he deserved. The elevator then screeched to a stop. Someone suggested she apologize. Once she did, the elevator continued its ride.

A Hotel or a Hospital?

Hotel Provincial, New Orleans, Louisiana

During the U.S. **Civil War** (1861–1865), there were not enough hospitals to take care of all the sick and injured soldiers. So other buildings had to be used as well. The Hotel Provincial was turned into one of these **temporary** hospitals. While the building is now a hotel again, some say its patients have never left.

Wounded Civil War soldiers outside a temporary hospital

Building number 5 is reported to be the spookiest section of the Hotel Provincial. Once, a hotel worker watched an entire scene from the past brought back to life there. As the elevator doors opened, he did not see the regular hallway. Instead, the bodies of bloody Civil War soldiers covered the floor. They moaned and cried for help, as if the Provincial was still their hospital.

Staff members aren't the only ones seeing strange spirits from the past. Guests have seen the ghosts of Civil War soldiers and doctors roaming the halls. Some sad souls reach out as if they need an arm to lean on. One girl stepped out of the shower and saw what looked like a pile of towels on the floor. Looking closer, she realized that they were bloody bandages and sheets. When she tried to pick them up, they disappeared.

Hotel Provincial

People have reported seeing bloodstains mysteriously appear and disappear on the beds in some rooms at the Hotel Provincial.

A Fiery Spirit

Old Bermuda Inn, Staten Island, New York

Martha Mesereau's husband was one of the many men who fought in the U.S. Civil War. Unfortunately, like many soldiers he was killed in battle. It is said that Martha's ghost still waits for him to return.

Old Bermuda Inn

The Old Bermuda **Inn** was originally the home of Martha Mesereau and her husband. It was in this lovely **mansion** that Martha found out the horrible news about her husband's death in the Civil War. Mad with **grief**, she locked herself in her room. Days passed without her eating anything. Slowly, Martha starved herself to death.

Since the house was turned into an inn, Martha's spirit has made itself known. There is a door to one of the upstairs rooms that often opens by itself. The staff has locked the door closed, only to find it open again.

Some nights after everyone has gone to bed, a single light turns on. Other times, fires are lit without any human help. Perhaps Martha wants her husband to know she's still waiting up for him.

Portrait of
Martha Mesereau

One of the strangest events at the inn took place when it was being **renovated**. Martha's portrait, which hangs in the front hall, suddenly burst into flames. Was Martha trying to let people know she didn't like the changes being made to her house?

A Stranger at the Inn

Jamaica Inn, Cornwall, England

The Jamaica Inn was built in 1750. **Smugglers**, **highway robbers**, and other criminals would often stop there. One of the inn's best-known ghosts is thought to have been killed by one of these troublemakers.

Jamaica Inn

Many years ago, a stranger entered the Jamaica Inn and ordered a drink. He may have been a sailor, a smuggler, or simply a tired traveler passing through. Shortly afterward, another man appeared. He and the stranger stepped outside. The mysterious stranger was never seen alive again. His dead body was found outside the next day.

Who was this stranger? No one knows for sure. Some say he still haunts the Jamaica Inn. People have reported seeing his ghost sitting on the stone wall outside the building. Many strange noises at the inn are thought to come from the ghost of the murdered stranger. Guests have heard footsteps where no one is walking. They have also heard conversations in a language they cannot understand. Is it the murdered stranger trying to let people know the truth about what happened years ago?

It has been a long time since people traveled by **stagecoach**. Some of the ghosts at the Jamaica Inn, however, still seem to travel that way. People have heard the sound of horses' hooves and the rattle of a **carriage** on the cobblestones. Yet when they go outside, no one is there.

The Worst Wedding Day

The Fairmont Banff Springs Hotel, Banff, Alberta, Canada

A wedding day is usually one of the happiest days of a person's life. For one woman at the Fairmont Banff Springs Hotel, this day was also her last. The ghost of this bride is still waiting to walk down the aisle.

The Fairmont Banff Springs Hotel

On her wedding day, the beautiful bride was dressed in a long white gown. The staircase at the Fairmont Banff Springs Hotel glowed with lighted candles. As the bride made her way down the stairs, however, something went terribly wrong.

According to some stories, her dress touched a candle and caught fire. Terrified, she tried to put out the flames and began to tumble down the staircase. Other stories say the poor woman just tripped on her dress. Whatever the reason, the bride fell down the stairs and died.

Guests of the Fairmont Banff Springs Hotel have since reported spotting the ghostly bride wandering the halls. She has also been seen on the stairs that led to her death. Others have seen this sad ghost waltzing in the ballroom. Still in her beautiful gown, she finally gets to dance at her wedding.

The Fairmont Banff Springs Hotel is also home to a ghostly **bellhop** named Sam. He **retired** in 1967 and died a few years after that. Yet his spirit still helps out guests. He has been known to unlock doors for those who've lost their keys.

The Captain Says Hello

The Olde Angel Inn, Niagara-on-the-Lake, Ontario, Canada

During the War of 1812, Americans fought the English in Canada and the United States. In May 1813, American soldiers captured the area around a Canadian inn that is now called the Olde Angel Inn. As American forces marched close to the building, most of the British left the area. One captain, however, made the mistake of trying to hide in the inn.

The Olde

ANGEL INN

★ GUEST ROOMS
★ FINE FOOD
★ ENGLISH PUB
★ WINE BAR

Americans fighting the British during the War of 1812

Captain Swayze assumed he was safe. He was hidden inside a wooden barrel in the inn's **cellar**. He thought he would just wait until the American soldiers left. Instead, the thrust of an American **bayonet** ended his life.

Today, when workers at the Olde Angel Inn hear footsteps in empty rooms, they assume it is just Captain Swayze. Without being seen, he opens doors and moves dishes around. His red-coated ghost appears in a mirror near the cellar where he died.

When Peter Ling bought the hotel in 1992, he was looking forward to meeting Captain Swayze. One night at 3:00 A.M. he seemed to get his wish. He woke to the sound of a crash. He soon saw that his lucky horseshoe had been pulled off the wall and thrown across the room. Perhaps it was Captain Swayze's way of introducing himself to the new owner.

Some guests at the inn have woken up to see Captain Swayze in their rooms. He floats up through the floor and stares at them while they lie in bed.

A Jealous Spirit

The Feathers Hotel, Ludlow, Shropshire, England

The ancient town of Ludlow is said to be the home of many ghosts. Ludlow Castle is haunted by the spirit of a woman who killed herself. On Market Street, the figure of a man in a black **cloak** floats near the place where he was murdered long ago. With so many ghosts in Ludlow, is it any wonder that the local hotel is haunted too?

The Feathers Hotel

The Feathers Hotel was built in the 1600s. Over the years, room 211 has become the home to a mysterious female ghost. She is kind to men but mean to women. When women have tried to sleep in the room, they often wake up feeling someone tugging at their hair.

One woman said her hair was yanked so hard that it pulled her out of bed. Her husband felt something different, however. Instead of a violent tug he felt a soft hand on his cheek. The couple eventually went back to sleep.

The ghost wasn't finished with the woman, however. When she awoke in the morning, her nightgown was soaking wet. Yet the rest of the bed was dry.

Why is the ghost in room 211 so mean to women? Unfortunately, the answer remains a mystery. So many guests have stayed at the Feathers Hotel that it is impossible to know just who the ghost once was—or why she is so jealous of other women.

A man dressed in clothes from the 1800s has been seen walking his dog from room to room at the Feathers Hotel. He doesn't use doors, however. To get from one room to another, this ghost and his **phantom** dog simply walk through the wall.

The Ghost of Room 218

The Crescent Hotel, Eureka Springs, Arkansas

In the late 1800s, many people believed that the water from Eureka Springs could cure their diseases. People who were ill traveled there from all over the United States, hoping to get better. Many of them stayed at the Crescent Hotel—a building that has been haunted since the time it was built.

The Crescent Hotel

Construction began on the Crescent Hotel in 1884. Within a year, it had its first ghostly guest. In 1885, a worker named Michael lost his balance and fell from the roof. He died in the area of the building that became room 218. It is said that his ghost plays tricks there.

Guests complain that Michael's ghost shakes them awake at night and slams doors. He pounds on the walls and turns the television on and off. The wife of one of the hotel's owners tried sleeping in room 218 and did not make it through the night. She came running out after seeing what looked like blood splashed all over the walls. Maybe she was dreaming. Or maybe Michael was just playing another ghostly prank in room 218.

During the early 1900s, the Crescent Hotel was home to a women's college. The death of one of its students remains a mystery. Did she fall or was she pushed from the fourth-floor deck? Her sad spirit is often seen in the beautiful hotel gardens.

The Fairmont Banff Springs Hotel
Banff, Alberta, Canada

A ghostly bride dances in her wedding dress.

The Olde Angel Inn
Niagara-on-the-Lake, Ontario, Canada

A British army captain haunts a Canadian inn.

Old Bermuda Inn
Staten Island, New York

A widow still waits for her husband to return from war.

St. James Hotel
Cimarron, New Mexico

A mean gambler still picks fights long after he was killed.

Queen Mary Floating Hotel
Port of Long Beach, California

The cries of ghostly sailors can be heard at this floating hotel.

Hotel Del Coronado
Coronado, California

Kate Morgan's ghost makes guests wonder just how she died.

The Crescent Hotel
Eureka Springs, Arkansas

The ghost of a workman plays tricks on guests in room 218.

Hotel Provincial
New Orleans, Louisiana

Ghosts remain at a hotel that was once a Civil War hospital.

Biltmore Hotel
Coral Gables, Florida

A murdered gangster still enjoys entertaining guests.

Around the World

The Feathers Hotel
Ludlow, Shropshire, England

A jealous spirit pulls the hair of women in room 211.

Jamaica Inn
Cornwall, England

A mysterious stranger arrives at an inn and stays forever.

Arctic Ocean

NORTH AMERICA

EUROPE

ASIA

Atlantic Ocean

AFRICA

Indian Ocean

Pacific Ocean

SOUTH AMERICA

AUSTRALIA

Southern Ocean

ANTARCTICA

Glossary

bayonet (bay-uh-NET) a long knife that can be attached to the end of a rifle

bellhop (BEL-hop) a person who works in a hotel carrying luggage and helping guests

carriage (KA-rij) a vehicle that has wheels, often pulled by horses

casino (kuh-SEE-noh) a room or building used for gambling

cellar (SEL-ur) a room in a building that is underground and is often used for storing things

Civil War (SIV-il WOR) the U.S. war between the Northern and Southern states that lasted from 1861–1865

cloak (KLOHK) a loose coat with no sleeves that is often worn to hide someone

docked (DOKT) placed in the landing area where ships load and unload goods

gangsters (GANG-sturz) people who are part of a group of criminals

grief (GREEF) great sadness

gunslingers (GUHN-*sling*-urz) people who are able to shoot a gun with great skill and speed

highway robbers (HYE-way ROB-urz) criminals who steal from people traveling on country roads

illegal (i-LEE-guhl) against the law

inn (IN) a small hotel

mansion (MAN-shuhn) a very large and grand house

military (MIL-uh-*ter*-ee) having to do with the armed forces

ocean liner (OH-shuhn LINE-ur) a large ship that can carry many people or lots of goods

outlaws (OUT-lawz) criminals who are running away from the law

phantom (FAN-tuhm) a ghost

pistol (PISS-tuhl) a small gun

renovated (REN-uh-*vate*-id) improved the condition of something

retired (ri-TYE-urd) stopped working forever, usually because of age

smugglers (SMUHG-lurz) people who secretly bring in or take out goods in a way that is against the law

speakeasy (SPEEK-*ee*-zee) a place that illegally sells alcoholic drinks

spirit (SPIHR-it) a supernatural creature, such as a ghost

stagecoach (STAYJ-*kohch*) a carriage pulled by horses

temporary (TEM-puh-*rer*-ee) lasting for a short period of time; not permanent

Bibliography

Belanger, Jeff. *The World's Most Haunted Places: From the Secret Files of Ghostvillage.com.* Franklin Lakes, NJ: New Page Books (2004).

Belanger, Jeff, ed. *Encyclopedia of Haunted Places: Ghostly Locales from Around the World.* Franklin Lakes, NJ: New Page Books (2005).

Blackhall, Susan. *Ghosts of New York.* San Diego, CA: Thunder Bay Press (2005).

Christensen, Jo-Anne. *Haunted Hotels.* Edmonton, Alberta, Canada: Ghost House Books (2002).

Coulombe, Charles A. *Haunted Places in America: A Guide to Spooked and Spooky Public Places in the United States.* Guilford, CT: The Lyons Press (2004).

Hauck, Dennis William. *Haunted Places: The National Directory.* New York: Penguin Books (2002).

Hauck, Dennis William. *The International Directory of Haunted Places.* New York: Penguin (2000).

Kermeen, Frances. *Ghostly Encounters: True Stories of America's Haunted Inns and Hotels.* New York: Warner Books (2002).

Mead, Robin. *Haunted Hotels: A Guide to American and Canadian Inns and Their Ghosts.* Nashville, TN: Rutledge Hill Press (1995).

Read More

Banks, Cameron. *America's Most Haunted.* New York: Scholastic (2002).

Holub, Joan. *The Haunted States of America.* New York: Aladdin (2001).

Wood, Ted. *Ghosts of the Southwest: The Phantom Gunslinger and Other Real-Life Hauntings.* New York: Walker & Company (1997).

Learn More Online

To learn more about haunted hotels, visit
www.bearportpublishing.com/ScaryPlaces

Index

About the Author

Sarah Parvis is a writer and editor in New York.
She lives in Brooklyn and loves ghost stories.